FOOD CHAINS

WHAT EATS WHAT IN A FOREST FOOD CHAIN

ILLUSTRATED BY ZACK MCLAUGHLIN

WRITTEN BY LISA J. AMSTUTZ

T0052869

PICTURE WINDOW BOOKS
a capstone imprint

Every plant and animal in a forest is part of a food chain. In a food chain, energy moves from one living thing to the next.

In a forest, the trees are the first link in a food chain. They reach toward the sun. Almost all food chains need the sun's energy.

producer

Producers use sunlight, water, nutrients, and air to make their own food.

Plop! An acorn falls from the tree. An acorn weevil spies a crack. The weevil chews the seed inside.

A consumer eats plants or animals for energy. An herbivore eats only plants.

consumer, herbivore

A hungry mouse spots the weevil. Crunch!
The mouse will save the acorn for later.
consumer,
omnivore

An omnivore eats both plants and animals.

A young snake coils nearby, waiting.

Gulp!

consumer, carnivore

A carnivore eats only other animals.

Its belly full, the snake finds a spot to rest.

consumer,
omnivore

Later a raccoon rambles down to the river.
It spots dinner and swipes. The snake makes a good meal.

The raccoon heads back to its den.
A bobcat waits quietly in the trees.

Pounce! The cat attacks.
consumer,
carnivore

The bobcat is a great hunter. But one day the bobcat is hurt in a fight with another cat. The wound is deadly.

A vulture feeds on parts of the bobcat's body.
consumer, scavenger
A scavenger eats mainly dead plants or animals.

Worms, bacteria, and fungi break down the rest. The decomposers return nutrients to the soil.

decomposers

Decomposers break down dead plants and animals. Their waste is used as nutrients by plants.

In spring an acorn sprouts. It uses the nutrients in the soil to grow.

A new oak tree reaches for the sun. And the food chain goes on.

FOOD WEB

You've seen a food chain in action. Now take a look at this temperate deciduous forest food web. A food web is made up of many food chains in one area.

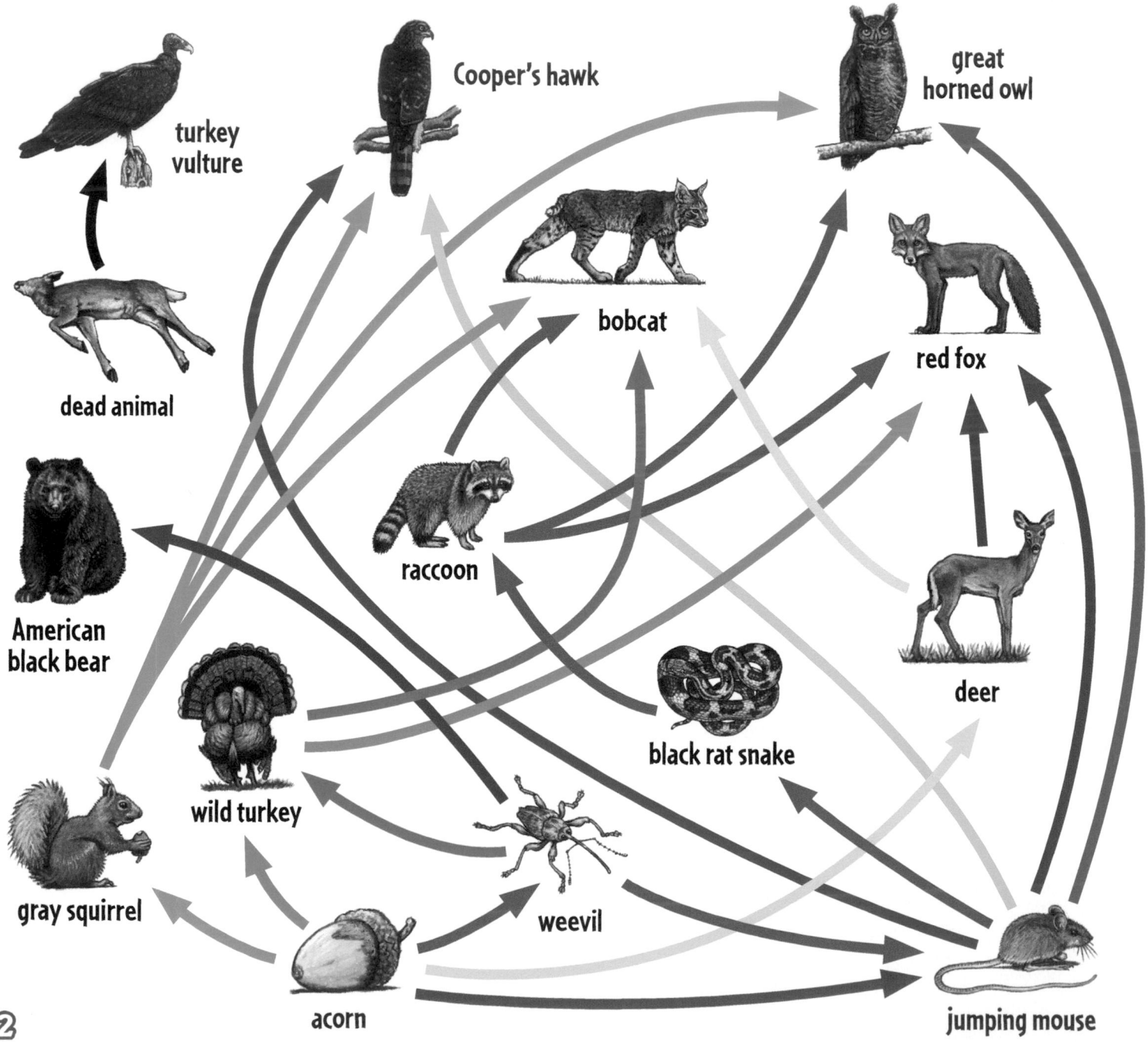